# This Book Belongs to:

.............................................

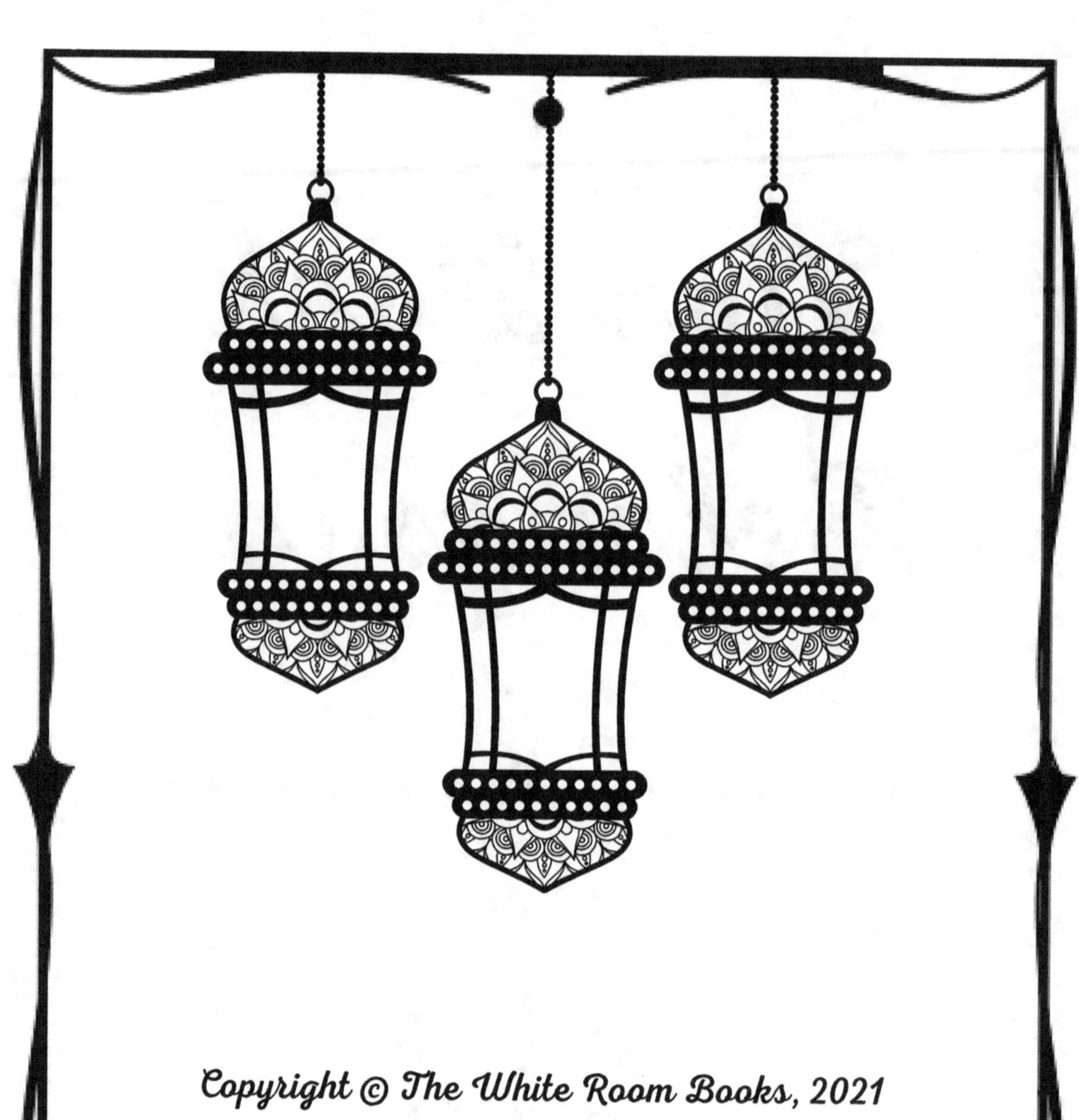

Copyright © The White Room Books, 2021
All rights reserved.

We hope you enjoy this book, and we would really appreciate your feedback/review on Amazon to help support us so we can keep creating more books!

بسم الله الرحمن الرحيم

# About Islam

- Islam is the world's second-largest religion with around 1.9 billion followers
- The followers of Islam are called Muslims
- All Muslims believe in one God whom they call **Allah**, which the Arabic name for God
- Islam is an Arabic word that means submission and comes from a word meaning peace
- Muslims consider Islam to be a **complete way of life**
- Islam was founded by Prophet Muhammad (Peace be upon him) in the Middle East over 1400 years ago
- Prophet Muhammad gave Allah's message to the people on Earth and introduced the faith of Islam
- The Quran is the Holy book of Muslims and it was revealed to Prophet Muhammad by Allah through the archangel Gabriel (Jibrīl)
- Muslims go to worship in a Mosque
- The Muslim holy day is Friday

# About Ramadan

- Ramadan is the holiest month in the Islamic calendar
- Ramadan is the 9th month of the Islamic calendar
- The term Ramadan comes from the Arabic meaning 'scorching heat'
- During Ramadan, Muslims do not eat or drink from sunrise to sunset, including water
- This is called fasting
- Fasting during Ramadan allows Muslims to devote themselves to their faith
- Ramadan started when Prophet Muhammad (PBUH) received the first verso of the Quran
- Ramadan lasts 29 or 30 days and begins with the sighting of the new moon and ends with another crescent new moon
- Muslims eat 'Suhoor' just before starting their fast and eat 'iftar' after ending their fast
- The festival of Eid-al-Fitr brings Ramadan to an end

# Importance of being mindful

- Exercising mindfulness can help discipline our minds and focus on our connection with Allah
- Mindfulness goes hand in hand with the pillars of faith and is clear from many examples from the prophet Muhammad's life
- Doing good deeds and having the right belief go hand in hand in Islam
- Happiness in Islam can be found performing acts of kindness or giving charity
- In this book, we have listed 30 different acts of kindness and mindfulness that you can perform over the course of Ramadan
- By performing these acts of kindness, you will be brought closer to Allah

# Basic glossary of Islamic terms

- **Allah**: The Arabic term for "God"
- **As-salaam Alaikum**: A common greeting used by Muslims around the world which means "peace be upon you" in Arabic. The response is Wa-Alaikum As-Salaam, "may peace be upon you too"
- **Ayah**: A verse in the Quran. Each surah or chapter varies in the number of ayat or verses that it has. The shortest chapter has 3 ayat and the longest has 286
- **Eid ul Fitr**: Celebration at the end of the month of Ramadan
- **Eid ul-Adha**: Celebration at the end of Hajj
- **Hadith**: Sayings or actions of the Prophet Muhammad that were recorded by his companions and later collected and preserved for the later generations
- **Kaaba**: Building in Mecca that is believed to be the first house of worship to God
- **Masjid**: The Arabic word for Mosque
- **Quran**: The Holy Book of Islam
- **Sunnah**: The example or practice of the Prophet Muhammad

# Hadith of the Day

Abu Ayub (may Allah be pleased with him) reported that the Prophet (peace and blessings be upon him) said, "Whosoever fasts in Ramadan and then follows it with fasting six days of Shawwal, it is as if he fasts forever." (Muslim)

# Mindful deed of the Day

**1** Help your family prepare Iftar

# Hadith of the Day

Abu Hurayrah reported that the Prophet (peace and blessings be upon him) said "Fasting is a shield; so when one of you is fasting he should neither indulge in obscene language nor should he raise his voice in anger. If someone attacks him or insults him, let him say: "I am fasting" (Muslim)

# *Mindful deed of the Day*

**2** Make your own
bed in the morning

# Hadith of the Day

Abu Hurayrah reported that the Prophet (peace and blessings be upon him) said,
The five (daily) prayers, and from one Friday prayer to the next, and from Ramadan to Ramadan are expiation for sins committed in between provided one stays away from the major sins.
(Al-Bukhari)

# Mindful deed of the Day

**3** Pray with your parents or family

# Hadith of the Day

Abu Hurayrah reported that the Prophet (peace and blessings be upon him) said, Whoever observes fasts during the month of Ramadan out of sincere faith and hoping to attain Allah's rewards, then all his past sins will be forgiven. (Al-Bukhari and Muslim)

# Mindful deed of the Day

**4** Save money and give it to charity

# Hadith of the Day

Abu Hurayrah reported that the Prophet (peace and blessings be upon him) said

Whoever stands (in the voluntary night prayer of) Ramadan out of faith and in hope of reward, his previous sins will be forgiven. (Al-Bukhari and Muslim)

# Mindful deed of the Day

**5** Feed the birds some seeds

# Hadith of the Day

Abu Hurayrah reported that the Prophet (peace and blessings be upon him) said

Whoever stands (in the voluntary night prayer) in Laylat Al-Qadr out of faith and in hope of reward, his previous sins will be forgiven. (Al-Bukhari)

**6** Learn a new Surah from the Quran

# Hadith of the Day

Abu Sa'id Al-Khudri (May Allah be pleased with him) reported that the Prophet (peace and blessings be upon him) said,

Anyone who fasts for one day for Allah's sake, Allah will keep his face away from the Hellfire for (a distance covered by a journey of) seventy years. (Al-Bukhari and Muslim)

# Mindful deed of the Day

**7** Do a chore in the house but don't tell anyone

# Hadith of the Day

Uthman ibn Abi Al-`Aas reported that the Prophet (peace and blessings be upon him) said, "Fasting serves as a shield from Hellfire." (An-Nasa'i and authenticated by Al-Albani)

# Mindful deed of the Day

**8** Smile at everyone and don't complain

# Hadith of the Day

Abdullah ibn 'Amr reported that the Prophet (peace and blessings be upon him) said,

Fasting and the Qur'an will intercede on behalf of Allah's servant on the Day of Judgment:

Fasting will say, "O my Lord! I prevented him from food and desires during the day, so accept my intercession for him."

And the Qur'an will say, "O my Lord! I prevented him from sleeping by night, so accept my intercession for him."

The intercession of both will thus be accepted. (Ahmad and authenticated by Al-Albani)

# Mindful deed of the Day

**9** Plant some seeds or a flower

# Hadith of the Day

Ibn ʿAbbas (may Allah be pleased with him) narrated:

"The Prophet was the most generous of all people, and he used to become more generous in Ramadan when (Angel) Gabriel met him. Gabriel used to meet him every night during Ramadan to revise the Qur'an with him. So, Allah's Messenger then used to be more generous than the fast wind."

(Al-Bukhari)

# Mindful deed of the Day

**10** Say Alhamdulillah after every meal

# Hadith of the Day

'A'ishah (May Allah be pleased with her) reported:

The Messenger of Allah (peace and blessings be upon him) used to strive more in worship during Ramadan than he strove in any other time of the year, and he would devote himself more (in the worship of Allah) in the last ten nights of Ramadan than he did in the earlier part of the month.

(Muslim)

# Mindful deed of the Day

**11** Donate a toy to charity

# Hadith of the Day

Abu Hurayrah reported:
The Prophet (peace and blessings be upon him) used to observe i'tikaf (spiritual retreat in a mosque) every Ramadan for ten days; in the year in which he passed away, he observed i'tikaf for twenty days. (Al-Bukhari)

# Mindful deed of the Day

**12** Invite a friend over for Iftar

# Hadith of the Day

Abu Hurayrah (may Allah be pleased with him) reported that the Prophet (peace and blessings be upon him) said: "When Ramadan enters, the gates of Paradise are opened, the gates of Hellfire are closed and the devils are chained." (Al-Bukhari and Muslim)

# Mindful deed of the Day

**13** Bake a cake for your neighbors

# Hadith of the Day

Umm Saleem (may Allah be pleased with her) reported that the Prophet (peace and blessings be upon him) said: "(The performance of) ʿUmrah during Ramadan is equal (in reward) to performing Hajj with me."
(Authenticated by Al-Albani)

# Mindful deed of the Day

**14** Listen to a dua before you go to sleep

# Hadith of the Day

Abu Hurayrah reported that the Messenger of Allah (peace and blessings be upon him) said:

There are two occasions of joy for a fasting person: one when he breaks his fast, and the other when he meets his Lord, and the (bad) breath (of a fasting person) is better in the sight of Allah than the fragrance of musk.

(Al-Bukhari)

# Mindful deed of the Day

**15** Help water the plants

# Hadith of the Day

Islam is based on Five Principles and observing Fast (according to Islamic Teachings) during the month of Ramadan is one of them,
(Al-Bukhari)

# Mindful deed of the Day

**16** Give your family hugs
and tell them how much
you appreciate them

# Hadith of the Day

The blessing of food is to wash hands at the beginning and washing after taking it.
(Miskhat)

# Mindful deed of the Day

**17** Pick up trash where you see it and put it in the bin

# Hadith of the Day

If anyone pledges to me that he will keep his tongue under control, guard his chastity, will not speak ill of others not indulge in slander or back-biting ... and similar sins, I shall assure him of Paradise.

(Al-Bukhari)

# Mindful deed of the Day

**18** Make sure you use 'thank you' and 'please' everytime today.

# Hadith of the Day

Those who are kind and considerate to Allah's creatures, Allah bestows His kindness and affection on them. Show kindness on the Earth so that Allah may be kind to you.
(Abu Dawud, Tirmidhi)

# Mindful deed of the Day

**19** Write a thank you letter to your parents and tell them why you love them

# Hadith of the Day

Do not quarrel with your brother Muslim, nor jest with him nor make a promise which you cannot keep.
(Tirmidhi)

# Mindful deed of the Day

**20** Do something kind for someone without them having to ask

# Hadith of the Day

The learned men are the successors of the Prophets. They leave behind knowledge as an inheritance. One who inherits it obtains a great fortune.
(Al-Bukhari)

# *Mindful deed of the Day*

**21** Learn and recite Surah Al-Qadr

This Surah celebrates the night when the first revelation of what would become the Qur'an was sent down to Earth

# Hadith of the Day

A man asked the Prophet, "O Messenger of Allah, who deserves the best care from me? The Prophet replied, "Your mother." The man asked, "Who then?" The Prophet said, "Your mother". The man asked again, "Who then?" The Prophet said "Your mother".
(Al-Bukhari)

# Mindful deed of the Day

**22** Take water and dates to your parents at Iftar today

# Hadith of the Day

The young should always say Salam to the old, the passer-by to the one sitting, and the small group to the large one.

(Al-Bukhari)

# *Mindful deed of the Day*

**23** Make sure you say As-salam Alaikum to everyone you meet

# Hadith of the Day

Eat and drink, give sadaqah and wear good clothes as long as these do not involve excess of arrogance.
(Nasai, Ibn Majah)

# Mindful deed of the Day

**24** Donate some clothes to charity or needy

# Hadith of the Day

Guarantee me six things and I shall assure you of Paradise: when you speak, speak the truth, keep your promise, discharge your trust, guard your chastity and lower your gaze and withhold your hands from highhandedness.

(Baihaqi)

# Mindful deed of the Day

**25** Make a dua list and pray for everyone

# Hadith of the Day

If a person does not refrain from lying and indecent activities (in Ramadhan), then Allah does not want that he should abstain from eating and drinking.
(Al-Bukhari)

**26** Help decorate the house for Eid

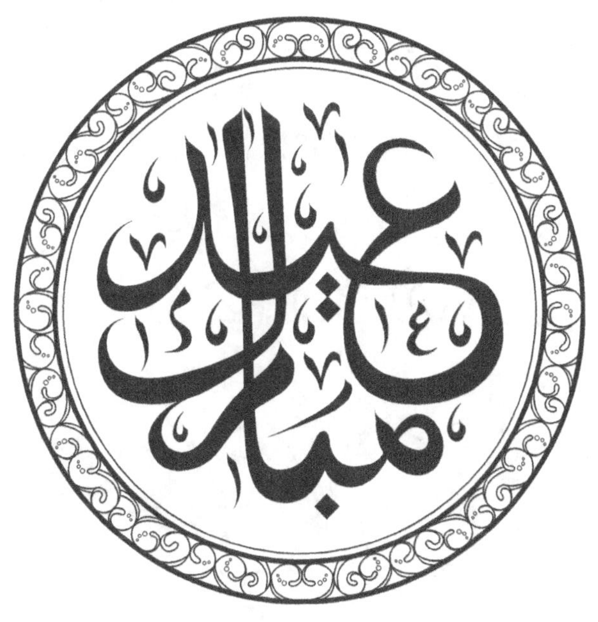

# Hadith of the Day

I heard Allah's Apostle saying, When you see the crescent (of the month of Ramadan), start fasting, and when you see the crescent (of the month of Shawwal), stop fasting; and if the sky is overcast (and you can't see it) then regard the month of Ramadan as of 30 days.
(Al-Bukhari)

# Mindful deed of the Day

**27** Write down all the things and people you are grateful for

# Hadith of the Day

The Prophet said, Whoever established prayers on the night of Qadr out of sincere faith and hoping for a reward from Allah, then all his previous sins will be forgiven; and whoever fasts in the month of Ramadan out of sincere faith, and hoping for a reward from Allah, then all his previous sins will be forgiven.

(Al-Bukhari)

# Mindful deed of the Day

**28** Buy or make some Eid gifts for your family

# Hadith of the Day

Zaid bin Thabit said, We took the Suhur with the Prophet . Then he stood for the prayer. I asked, What was the interval between the Suhur and the Adhan? He replied, The interval was sufficient to recite fifty verses of the Qur'an.
(Al-Bukhari)

# Mindful deed of the Day

**29** Make and send Eid cards

# Hadith of the Day

The Prophet said, If somebody eats or drinks forgetfully then he should complete his fast, for what he has eaten or drunk, has been given to him by Allah.
(Al-Bukhari)

# Mindful deed of the Day

**30** Apologise and own up to any mistakes you make

EID
Mubarak